The Employee is Always Right

The Employee is Always Right

A Guide to Customer Service,

Employee Satisfaction, and

Competitive Advantage

An Avason Consulting Publication

Written By:

Kurt V. Spady, MBA

ISBN: 978-0-9936673-1-2

Visit our website at http://www.avasonconsulting.com

Book design by Janelle Spady

Library and Archives Canada has catalogued this edition as follows:

Spady, Kurt V., 1983 –

The Employee is Always Right – A Guide to Customer Service, Employee Satisfaction, and Competitive Advantage

/ By Kurt Spady

Published and distributed by Avason Consulting Corp.

PO BOX 25059

Red Deer, Alberta, Canada T4R 2M2

Telephone - (403) 596-8389

Email – customerservice@avasonconsulting.com

DEDICATION

This book is dedicated to Ava and Jackson, for whom I would like to leave the world a better place.

ACKNOWLEDGMENTS

I would like to acknowledge the perceptiveness of those organizations that choose to put their employees first, and moreover, those organizations that choose not to for inspiring me to write this book.

Table of Contents

Preface xi

CHAPTER 1 1

Employee Customer Service 1

CHAPTER 2 11

Banal Platitudes – Stop Using Them 11

CHAPTER 3 17

Employee Motivation 17

Chapter 4 23

Employer Motivation 23

CHAPTER 5 29

Customer Motivation 29

Chapter 6 35

Self-Awareness 35

CHAPTER 7 39

The Customer is Always Right 39

Chapter 8 53

Employee Attraction and Retention 53

CHAPTER 9 57

Marketing and Branding 57

CHAPTER 10 65

Change Management 65

CHAPTER 11 75

Unions and Collective Agreements 75

CHAPTER 12 79

The Bottom Line 79

CHAPTER 13 83

Conclusions 83

References 87

About the Author 91

Index 93

YOU HAVE LIKELY HEARD the saying, "The Customer is Always Right". You have also likely heard the variations "The Customer is Not Always Right BUT They Are Still The Customer", "We Put Customers First", "We Value Our Customers", etc.

Have you ever heard these types of sayings about employees?

Probably not, or at least it's not as prevalent and obvious in a company's advertising, marketing, or branding efforts. Most of those sayings sound like "our employees receive competitive wages and benefits, opportunities for training, etc." In fact, I challenge you to find a job advertisement that doesn't contain some type of variation of that pitch. Maybe the airline West Jet with their saying, that "our employees are owners too", would qualify as an uncommon reference to employee service. However it could be suggested that company is an exception to the rule, and in more areas than one.

It is the purpose of this book to illustrate the importance of the idea that employers need to start viewing their employees with the same type of respect and urgency that they view their customers. Organizations would benefit not only by having happier employees, but that this would also translate into great customer service, as well as high quality products and service outputs. This in turn creates a competitive advantage for the organization in the marketplace.

In the following pages various idea points will be illustrated to help convince you of this conclusion, with supporting research and data along with a logical construct that will prove that this is the case.

These ideas did not come to be overnight; they come from many years of studying and experiencing various working environments in which employees are treated very differently.

The underlying ideas for this approach are also not new and are backed up by various research relating to employee motivation, empowerment, customer service, change management, organizational behavior, and brand management (among other areas of the organizational management discipline).

The point is that it will come across as common sense, which it is. But we all know what they say about common sense, that it's not very common. This is not a bad thing, nor is it being suggested that it is so plainly simple that every organization should know this concept of "the employee is always right". Often it is the case that solutions to very complex problems (and this is one) are right in front of us, the challenge is putting the solutions together in an intuitive way that works.

You will not find an organization that says they do not value their employees or their customers. It is the actions within these two arenas that speak louder than words and employees, like customers, will vote with their feet.

Both sides of the idea will be presented throughout the book, with rebuttal statements included to help assist with critical thinking towards some of the thoughts and ideas presented.

CHAPTER 1

Employee Customer Service

"The employer generally gets the employees they deserve"

-J. Paul Getty

Here is a situation that seemed very counterintuitive at the time, but over time it began to make more and more sense.

The situation unfolded as follows:

- An irate customer enters a grocery store with a competitor's brand of stale-dated sour cream in hand wanting restitution. In this situation the customer was completely wrong; they had clearly not purchased the product at the store but at a competitors, as it was their own house brand. This was in the early days of my experience with customers and employee customer service and I include it here to help analogize some of the ideas that we will be looking at in the following sections.

The solution was as follows:

- Refund the customer the money, engage them in conversation and have someone get a new container of sour cream or walk the customer to the product if they so desire.

A rebuttal statement you may have could be:

"But that customer is wrong, they didn't buy it here, they have no receipt, how is this the right thing to do? We are now out the money for the cost of the sour cream, and the staff time spent

1

helping that customer, which could have been spent helping customers that are actually buying product in our store."

The rationale for this approach is as follows:

For the few dollars that the sour cream cost the thinking was that this was a small price to pay for the chance to wow a customer and create repeat business. If this customer left satisfied and returned to the store or bought items on their way out, it was well worth the cost and staff time to replace the sour cream.

Lifelong customers are worth big money to any company or brand. For example, as the Pareto Principle sates, approximately 20% of an organizations' customers are generating about 80% of the revenue.

Do you know what else is worth a lot to an organization?

A lifetime employee.

We will address some of these factors later in the book but for now consider the costs of employee turnover such as lost productivity due to transition, posting or advertising for the position, interviews and the entire hiring process, training, lost knowledge etc. There have been various studies conducted on what this costs an organization (some will be cited here). Most of them contain some subjectivity, or depending on your industry they might not be applicable. When you do the math you will quickly see that this is an issue for employers, and you'll find to what extent it is an issue for your particular organization.

Ballinger et al. (2011) cites a US Labor Statistics report that indicates 30% of workers are staying with an employer for less than two years, and more than half are leaving before the 5 year mark. Direct costs of recruiting new hires are also cited at being between 25% and 500% of an employee's salary (Ballinger et al., 2011). Again, think about this in terms of having to advertise and hire for the position, lost knowledge, resources required to train someone new, lost productivity from the gap in the position, and lost productivity from training. Ballinger et al. (2011) cites an example in which General Mills claims that the loss of a senior marketing manager could cost the organization millions of dollars.

Cascio (2012) cites a Manpower survey that indicated that 75% of Chief HR officers reported that employers voluntarily lost some of their most high performing employees in 2011/12.

A 2008 study shows that companies that lay off 10% of their workers in any given year can expect a 50% spike of voluntary turnover that ranges from 10-15% (Cascio, 2012).

Ballinger et al. (2011) also discusses the idea of how organizational networks are impacted by employee turnover. Think of it in terms of not just looking at the operational or technical impacts of the position, but the social and organizational cultural impacts as well. For example, will other employees feel satisfied and secure in their jobs if a third of people hired are leaving within two years?

Ballinger et al. (2011) makes the point that it is simply not possible to replace a long term employee. Even if there is a similar skills profile, it takes time for the employee to demonstrate and the employer or manager to understand the person's expertise, as well as build trust and a relationship with that person (Ballinger et al., 2011). There is no way to truly know a person simply from a resume or an interview process. Even if it was, that person may act differently when put into a different environment. So someone that you knew did their jobs well and fit well into the social and cultural fabric of the organization, would take a long time or be impossible to replace.

In summary of the cost of employee turnover, employers have not fully recognized the true costs of losing key people, and do not have an in depth awareness of what it takes to keep them (Ballinger et al., 2011).

A way to start looking at your employee turnover is to measure it over the past 5 years as a benchmark. You can then follow Cascio's (2012) suggestions of looking at what turnover exists for industry competitors, report your turnover rates to your executive team, then calculating the costs of separating, replacing, and training employees to show the dollars saved and the costs avoided as a result of a low employee turnover rate.

It is also important to note that there should be some level of turnover in any organization. The suggested percentages can be within a wide range, but the underlying idea is that if you have a 0% turnover rate you are saying that everyone you have hired that is in their position is a perfect fit for their position and the organization. This is unlikely, as people tend to have career goals or end up being a mismatch for the organization or for the position they are in. For example, there are likely many industries and businesses where a turnover rate of 20% annually would be considered quite healthy.

The appropriate rate of turnover is very industry dependent, and dependent on other factors such as the labor market and economic conditions in the area. In any situation it is hard to justify turnover rates where three quarters or more of your employees are leaving within a year. Some seasonal businesses have high turnover but it is important to see what this is costing as it may be more beneficial, and by a high margin, to work to keep those turnover rates lower.

These employees that will potentially leave your organization within a short time serve your customers. If these employees are new and have little experience in the industry, or if you have not orientated them properly, they are less likely to perform for the organization in terms of delivering a high level of customer satisfaction.

Let's contrast the story at the beginning of this chapter, the customer with the competitor's sour cream, with one in which an employee comes in late to work.

The situation unfolds as follows:

- An employee comes into work 20 minutes late for their shift and does not say anything to anyone but simply begins their work.

4

The solution may be as follows:

- They are clearly in the wrong, they did not give any notice, and it is decided that they will not be paid for the 20 minutes they were late. You call the employee to your office and inform them of this.

If you don't work, you don't get paid. Sounds fair, right?

The question I would suggest you consider asking yourself is:

What is that 20 minutes worth to you?

You can either create a situation where the employee will be put in a position to defend themselves (it is likely they will have a good reason why they are late), or you can give them the benefit of the doubt.

Do you trust that the situation was legitimate, are you ever late for a good reason?

If you create a negative consequence for that employee, your relationship and trust could be negatively impacted over an issue of 20 minutes. Think about how much longer it takes to rebuild trust once broken, if repairable at all. You could even argue that the staff time to address this issue is worth far more than the 20 minutes of employee salary.

A rebuttal statement you may have could be:

"But wait, if I start letting people come in late, everyone will start coming in late. And if I allow people to be 20 minutes late, people might start showing up 30 minutes or an hour late. I need to draw the line and employees need to know that they are expected to show up to work on time."

A possible rationale is as follows:

It is unlikely that everyone will start to come in late. Here is an analogy that we can use to think about this:

There are ways to stop all theft (by employees or anyone), by placing armed security guards at the front of the building and strip searching everyone going in and out. Is it a reality that if you don't have armed guards at the door everyone will steal office supplies?

Again, not likely (and you probably don't do strip searches of everyone that walks in and out of your building).

Another rebuttal statement could be:

"Well, why don't we have searches? There is some theft and this would put an end to it."

Again, a similar rationale could explain this:

Similarly I would ask you to consider what a few pens taken home by accident or someone showing up a few minutes late is worth to you?

You could discipline the employee, who will always have a good excuse for being late, or taking a pen (whether it is the truth or not), or build trust in that relationship. If that employees takes their coffee break later than scheduled to help a customer, goes above and beyond to get their team what they need, is it worth it? Conversely if that same employee leaves an unattended customer because they know that their manager will scold them for not taking their break on time, this is less than ideal customer service.

Another rebuttal statement could be:

"But if I let people take their breaks whenever they want to it will be chaos and people will take advantage."

Part of this is about linking outcomes with expectations. Is the idea behind your business model and your source of competitive advantage in the marketplace that everyone starts and leaves on time, or that the customer is served? Is the goal to makes sure everyone takes their breaks at the scheduled time, or that the customer is served? If the breaks get taken at different times and the customer is still served does it matter? How much time did you spend on that employee being 20 minutes late when you should have been following up on a customer issue, walking the shop floor, checking in on the progress of a new product development?

Also, part of this idea about employee customer service is about assuming positive intent. As per our sour cream example, do you think that customer was intentionally trying to pull one over on the store by getting a refund on their sour cream? Did that late employee intentionally arrive late, calculating their every move in their morning ritual in order to try to ruin everything for the organization? No.

Think about how you treat your customers, and why you don't treat your employees the same way?

If you view your employees to be as valuable as your customers (and you should), are you providing excellent employee service?

Employee service sounds like a funny term but when you think about it, that's exactly what it is. What's interesting is why the concept does not flow as easily from the advertising offices of businesses. We see certain companies doing this, but it should be the majority.

The following is an unfortunate position that many managers, organizational leaders, and fellow employees have taken towards newcomers to the job market:

"Young people today have no work ethic or loyalty; they think they are owed something."

This is often attributed to a shift in the new generation of workers seeking more of a work-life balance.

Cogin (2012), states that it would likely be agreeable that no initiative aimed at enhancing an employee's quality of life would be accepted by everyone, and that workplaces are becoming increasingly diverse. Cogin (2012) also cites a study that indicates that in organizations with 500 or more employees, 58% of HR professionals reported conflict between younger and older workers due to each groups varying perceptions on things like work ethic and work-life balance.

The current workforce contains at least 4 generations, spanning more than 60 years in age, and include categories labeled Traditionalists, Baby Boomers, Generation X, and Generation Y (Cogin, 2012).

It should also be noted that this type of generational analysis occurs throughout the world and by various types of people and organizations. This results in a variety of labels (for example millennials versus generation Y), and dates or periods of time that overlap. Essentially how these are classified is that a generation is a group that shares both a span of birth years as well as a set of world views grounded in defining social or historical events that happened during that generations formative years (Mannheim, 1922/24 as cited in Cogin, 2012).

Compounding age differences are cultural, ethic, language, gender, and a variety of other factors that have an impact on how people perceive the world, and their value systems. Add to that people's own preferences for music, forms of communication, what they like to eat, what they can eat, health issues, and we have a very diverse group of people working in workplaces today.

Would you have a similar response to a customer that:

- Needed your assistance to find a product (or an employee that needs your help to get trained and orientated to the organization)?

- Asked you to come to complete a job in their home at a certain day and time that works with their schedule (or an employee that needs some flexibility in their working schedule)?

- Thought about shopping at another store because they were unsatisfied with the level of service that they received from you (or an employee that is considering working at another company because they don't feel their needs have been met)?

- Expects a high level of service and for you to cater to them (an employee that expects more than just a paycheck)?

These questions are rhetorical, but if you feel differently ask yourself what the consequences of your decision would be, and then is that decision the best for your business?

There are customers as well as employees that are not good for your business and you may have to ask them to leave. But likely the majority of employees and customers are good for business. As such your organizational processes and procedures should reflect best practice and positive intent on the preposition that customers and employees are looking to help your organization to be successful. This will result in lifelong beneficial relationships being developed.

Employers may demand hard work and loyalty and believe they are owed this. However, if the employer did not put any hard work into training employees (throw them in the deep end and see if they can swim), or won't give employees a benefits package until they have worked for them for three months (they want the employee to show loyalty first before they invest in them), an employer can't be surprised when employees demonstrate the same types of attitudes in return.

Employee Service and Customer Service are both important to an organizations ability to thrive and grow in an increasingly globalized and competitive marketplace.

CHAPTER 2

Banal Platitudes – Stop Using Them

"You can observe a lot just by watching"

-Yogi Berra

Platitude Definition:

> - A trite or banal remark or statement, especially one expressed as if it were original or significant

Here is an example of a banal platitude:

"Our organization is committed to honesty, transparency, good communication, accountability, fiscal responsibility, and leadership."

It sounds like a good list, but if you really think about it, these words mean different things to different people. So really, the words in and of themselves don't mean anything.

Organizations trying to determine their strategic plan will often go through the same steps:

1. <u>Where are we now:</u> people list problems like poor communication, lack of transparency, lack of time, lack of budget, lack of staff and other resources.

2. <u>Where are we going:</u> people will describe a desired future state, typically including many suggestions for people in the IT department.

3. <u>How are we going to get there:</u> increased communication, transparency, better time management, more staff training and put in a request for a bigger budget.

Then the same meeting will happen again next year, with new employees and a similar list or individual departments may complete the exercise as well.

The ability to turn these generic statements into tangible action items is accomplished by creating them with some specificity, matrices, realism, and timelines.

A popular acronym for this approach is to make the goals SMART:

S   – Specific
M   – Measurable
A   – Achievable
R   – Relevant
T   – Timely

For example, the first step is to have someone that is assigned specific duties for the action plan, specifying what they are to do and by when, making sure the task or project is achievable with existing resources, and set a timeline for completion.

We see various clichés or common sayings when we hear politicians speaking, talking a lot without really saying anything that could be considered SMART, as per our acronym.

For example:

"I care about my employees as they are the foundation of this organization, without them we would not be where we are today. Our customers are priority number 1 and we are willing to go the extra mile to serve them etc. etc."

Replace employees and customers with constituents and you will probably hear something close to that in the next political campaign from your district representative.

Let's look at some research so that we can link specific goal setting around some of the general platitudes mentioned, and see how we can create stronger levels of employee service within an organization.

Kliener (2000) wrote a commentary on Peter Drucker's book *Management Challengers for the 21st Century,* and suggested that everyone is a manager, as so much of our lives is facilitated or takes place through an organization. He goes on to suggest that as we move more towards knowledge work, that people will be forced to manage and choose how they engage in their own careers. As we have seen from traditional management theory, people in general will be more productive if they have autonomy over their work and their work-life balance.

Kliener (2000) goes on to suggest that this new state of employee management and knowledge work causes competition to move not just across national boundaries, but entire industrial categories, as highlighted by Drucker's book.

Kliener (2000) agrees with, and cites several sources, that state the idea that until the current traditional hierarchical management structure ceases to exist, that this newly flattened organizational structure may exist only as a platitude within organizations.

As stated, it is very easy to suggest that management and employees (as new managers of their own lives and careers), must be flexible in order to survive and thrive in the new global marketplace. It is another thing altogether to see this idea executed, which according to Kliener's article and those that he cited, will occur in the next generation of organizational managers.

Think about what Kliener's ideas on Peter Drucker's book means to you. If the new generation of employees are to be empowered knowledge workers, how will you assist them in managing what they do? Would it ever be ok to tell them they are wrong in how they choose to perceive things or approach projects? How can you ensure that SMART goals are being set for the organization?

A rebuttal response you may have to this idea could be:

"But employees might be making decisions that are wrong, there is no substitute for experience and that is typically what people need to have in order to be managers"

A proposed rationale would be:

Experience is valuable, but the question should be asked, in all of your years of experience have you ever encountered a situation that was exactly the same? Probably not. Yes, it is agreed that you develop certain skills over time, but those are unique skills to you and have been developed as a result of the experiences that you have had with certain projects.

Here are some additional banal statements that are often heard when referencing what it is that constitutes a good employee:

"There is no substitute for experience, good attitude, hard work, and loyalty, etc. etc."

A lot of these things are meaningless terms that are designed to describe what is required to get to the goal, to get from one place to another within the organization. The truth is that in order to get to a goal, the answer is different for everyone and this has been shown to be so. There is no cookie cutter mold for the perfect employee or leader for every situation. So why pretend that there is? Focus on specific goals instead of meaningless subjective attributes that people need to possess that don't really lend themselves to anything other than frustrating everyone. It's impossible to always get it "right", or "perfect" or to get a "10" on a performance evaluation if you have to guess what is acceptable as per someone else's perspective.

There are various general styles that have been adapted as potentially someone's "dominant" leadership style. Shaeffer (2002) outlines some of them in his leadership journey as a CEO, and describes being a leader not as a certain state, but a journey. The styles are outlined as follows:

Autocratic – Shaeffer (2002) describes this top down approach not as a leader who bullies others, but as the managerial equivalent of an emergency situation, where a surgeon is forced to do whatever it takes to save a patient's life. This is an excellent description of the ideal place to exert this type of leadership style. Can you think of some situation where this type of leadership style, that requires direct supervision and close control of employees and their actions, might not be the most appropriate approach?

Participative – Shaeffer (2002) describes his experience with this leadership style as one he adapted when the autocratic orders would not get the job done, as the organization was too large. Participative leadership would need to be implemented where the CEO would be given enough information from employees to make important strategic decisions, but where implementation would be undertaken by front line managers (Liket as cited in Shaeffer, 2002). Is it easy for you to let go of control? Can you think of ways that you can start to do this when working with others in your organization?

Reformer – This type of leader will demonstrate what is possible, and stubbornly try to make the world and the organization a better place (Shaeffer, 2002). Shaeffer (2002) also cites that he was able to realize that he as a leader could create real, industrial scale change.

The Shaeffer case of his leadership journey is a good example of someone not fitting into a box in terms of leadership style and needing to adapt to the environment. He ends his article by stating that the demands of the marketplace shaped who he was as a leader, and conversely you could argue that who some leaders are or were, (think Steve Jobs, Henry Ford, Bill Gates, Thomas Edison), shaped the marketplace.

Some other general leadership categories are the Paternalistic Leader, Democratic, Laissez-Faire, Transactional, and Transformational leadership types. Take these for what you will as they are simply definitions and not actual types of people walking around. However it does help, from an academic standpoint, to start thinking about each individualized component and how they fit together for yourself.

Spreier (2006) defines 6 leadership styles as Directive, Visionary, Affiliative, Participative, Pacesetting, and Coaching.

Spreier (2006) suggests that in the short term ambition and goal setting leaders have shown a great level of productivity, but that over the long term these characteristics could damage the performance of an organization. Can you think of some reasons why this might be?

Beltrami (2011) writes that these types of platitudes have developed into "industry codes" that are then re-disseminated to stakeholder groups. Think about this in your own organization or even department compared to another place where you have worked. Every organization, industry and even departments within organizations and industries can develop general, banal, platitudinous (see what I did there) ways of saying the same thing, while saying little to nothing at all.

Beltrami (2011) gives examples of certain areas within the organization where these platitudes are most likely to occur, being ethical codes, overstated performance claims, disclaimers, and compliance codes.

Set SMART goals to increase the level of employee service within your organization. This will be a foundational starting point and will lead to similarly defined goals for customer service, output levels, areas of growth and all other areas that you want to focus on in your organization.

CHAPTER 3

Employee Motivation

"To win in the marketplace you must first win in the workplace."

- Douglas Conant

Research shows that on the whole, employees are motivated more by intrinsic factors than extrinsic ones. Think of your own self, would you rather have more money, regardless of how you were treated by your employer, or be treated exceptionally well for a lower wage?

An interesting contrast to this is what can often be observed in the behavior of professional athletes.

For example many professional athletes are icons in their community. People admire them everywhere they go, they make millions of dollars, who could ask for more? We see players all the time moving for larger contracts, moving their families and going to new markets, all for more money. Some might say it's not the money that's important, it's what the money means.

I attended a speaker series where Brian Burke (2014) was speaking, who at the time was the President of Hockey operations for the Calgary Flames in Alberta, Canada. He mentioned that the single biggest factor in terms of getting players to play hockey in Canada, was the high taxes. I find this interesting because a hockey player, for example, in Calgary would be a local hero, and a player in Florida (where there is no state tax), would be a relative unknown. Mr. Burke mentioned that players love to play hockey in Florida.

Much of these decisions could be attributed to individual motivation, and that athletes only have a short number of years to play. Many are not interested in being celebrities (which I imagine presents its own unique challenges). But it could be suggested that the idea of a child going to the store to buy a jersey with your name on the back would have a high degree of intrinsic value for an individual.

Nicholoson (2003), writes on employee motivation in that it is easy to motivate and energize employees that want to be motivated, but how can you address those that don't? He also cites that few executives are very adept at rallying the troops (Nicholson, 2003). Think about that statement in your own life and career. What percentage of people have you found to be truly great as gifted leaders?

Nicholoson (2003) also cites that you cannot motivate other people, only they can motivate themselves. It is also the job of a manager or leader to create circumstance where that natural motivation will surface and be channeled towards goal achievement.

Think about that idea for a moment, that you cannot motivate people only they can motivate themselves. For example, is the gift card that you are giving out as a prize motivating people, or are they motivated to get the gift card? It's an important distinction in that if what Nicholson says is true, you have not motivated anyone, only created the condition for which the employee is willing to motivate themselves.

I remember hearing a professional fighter say that because of what has happened to them in their life, they go into the ring excited to win instead of being afraid to lose. That statement sticks with me as I think, although a simple and seemingly common sense statement, that this individual now has a more positive orientation towards their work because of their perception of what is happening. They are in a position to benefit, rather than in a position to lose.

You might not manage professional fighters (or maybe you do), but the key then is to find out what circumstances will best create the environment for employee motivation for your group of employees. And it is important to remember that they will not be motivated by what you choose, they will be motivated by what they choose to be motivated by.

A key point to remember that also sounds like common sense, is that everyone is different. Simply applying blanket "motivating factors" for a group of employees will not address their individual motivations. Many managers and employers are looking at their own motivators, for example more production, more profits, employee loyalty etc. In extreme cases, if the employee does not agree to be motivated by these same factors, if they don't like it, they can either choose to leave or be pushed out of the organization.

Nicholson (2003) writes on this point in terms of the notion of "de-centering". This describes when individuals move beyond their own self-centered perception of the world, towards an understanding that people's values, needs, etc. will be different.

For example something a manager or fellow employee might say is:

"If the lazy employee could simply work harder then I wouldn't have to yell at them all the time."

Whereas if there was less yelling the employee may begin to work harder in the more positive work environment.

Another example, if a manager's idea is that work should stay at work and home should stay at home, this may be in a stark contrast to what an employee believes should be the case. I have heard several arguments towards this example including:

"You have to leave work at work and home at home. That is the only way to be an effective manager."

"It is not realistic to think that a human being can simply leave their emotions at the door of the office. People are emotional and stressors both at home and at work will be factors in their performance and experiences at work."

"Yes that's true, but why should someone's personal problem be my problem at work?"

It might be the reality, either directly or indirectly, that either of these things will be the case and it all depends on the individuals involved in terms of what orientation towards the situation will be successful.

An example is a death in the family. One employee might feel you don't care about them if you don't ask about it and see how they are doing, etc. A different employee might tell you to stop talking to them about it because they don't want to have to discuss it at work and live with it at home.

This relates to the concept of empathy as well, when we attempt to "put ourselves in someone else's shoes" in order to better understand their viewpoint or perception of the world.

For example, is the late employee sleeping in all the time, or does their spouse have cancer and maybe "being on time for work" has fallen to a lower point in terms of that employees priorities. As a manager do you care? Should you care?

It's a case where we are looking at "symptoms of success" rather than focusing on those things that we are looking for in terms of organizational outcomes as an end result. Are we concerned an employee is on time, or that they have a healthy home and work-life balance in order to meet organizational targets long term.

Herzberg (2003) has written foundational research related to motivators, in particular the Two-Factor Theory. As a summary of the Two-Factor Theory, people are motivated by intrinsic motivators, and external hygiene factors. For example the ability to learn and grow with an organization would be an internal motivator, and salary would be a hygiene factor. Also related to the Two-Factor theory is that employees that are not satisfied are not dissatisfied, there is simply no satisfaction, or "the opposite of job dissatisfaction is not job satisfaction, but no job dissatisfaction" (Herzberg, 2003). Hertzberg (2003) relates the application of hygiene factors in the context of motivating people as a "kick in the pants" motivator, or KITP. Herzberg (2003) discusses why KITP motivators are not motivation because if you have to make someone do something, you will have to make them do it again. What you want is someone who will motivate themselves to do the task.

Employee motivation is not something that we will attempt to fully understand in this book. It is very complicated and decades of research and application have been undertaken to get a more comprehensive grasp on what motivates people.

For our purposes it's important to consider that everyone is motivated differently, and it is important to attempt to understand those motivations before jumping to conclusions or taking action that may be counter-productive.

It is also important to understand that you cannot motivate someone, that they can only motivate themselves and to think about how you will create those environments and relationships that will foster this.

The third and final point to remember is that extrinsic motivators, or hygiene factors, have a limited impact on their ability to motivate employees. Think of the prospect of getting a raise, at first it's exciting, and then a short period later you forget about it or start thinking about the next one.

Find out what motivates your employees and create an environment that will expose and channel these motivations. Employees serve the customers, make the company money, and are a large source of competitive advantage for an organization in the marketplace.

Also important to the concept of employee motivation is the labeling of "problem employees."

Nicholson (2003) cites the 80/20 rule (the Pareto Principle), in that 20% of your employees will take up 80% of a managers time and energy. Think about this for yourself or even if you are an employee, are there those 20% of people that you work with or encounter in a day taking up 80% of your time, energy and thought?

Nicholson (2003) also makes an important point in that these "problem" individuals can only motivate themselves, and this involves removing barriers for them to do so, which may likely also include your own attitude towards them.

Also, I have noticed that no one is ever the problem employee, for example no one would ever admit that or see themselves as a problem employee. Similarly, in management training sessions everyone is quick to point out that micro-management is a poor choice of management style, but we never find the micro-manager. It's always someone else who does the micro-managing and it is similarly difficult to find a self-identified problem employee.

Nicholson (2003) gives a good explanation for this that I think makes sense, that because everyone's motivational drivers are unique, that everyone has a different idea about what is "reasonable" behavior.

In effect there really are no problem employees, but only a mismatch between motivational drivers, value systems, and experiences. It's an easy thing to say and a hard thing to do but with the ideas in this chapter you should be able to start thinking about how your employee's motivation impacts your ability to provide employee service.

Chapter 4

Employer Motivation

"You do not lead by hitting people over the head – that's assault, not leadership."

- Dwight D. Eisenhower

It is important for employees, customers, and especially employers themselves to consider what motivates an employer, and the self-interest of those acting on behalf of the organization. It is also important to consider short term and long term effects of employer decisions guided by either short term or long term motivation.

For example, it could be suggested that it is in an employer's best interest to get the most productivity out of an employee for the least cost. In the short term that could mean pressuring them to working unpaid overtime, taking safety risks, working long hours, etc. But over the long term this may mean a less productive employee, or an employee that leaves the organization.

Another example could be where an organization strategically attempts to have the lowest dollar per labor hour possible for a job. It could be suggested that you get what you pay for in some of these situations.

Here are some questions to consider:

Is long term growth and sustainability created by paying your employees the lowest wage possible? How do you feel about customers that want to pay you the lowest amount possible?

Do organizations offer things like great compensation and benefits, flexible work hours etc. because they want to be good "citizens", or because it generates profits? Does intent matter?

Does your employer have formal contingency planning for things like life events, or is it more reactionary?

What is your organizations or your employer's stance on these questions? Have you seen examples of cause and effect related to some of the above situations?

These are all important considerations in terms of looking at an employer's motivation related to employee service.

Let's look at some research related to employer motivation and employee service:

Drago, Wooden & Black (2009) conducted a study where they investigated whether work hour preferences changed with life events. In general the study suggested yes, and that in fact in many cases the amount of hours worked in the labor market corresponded to these events and corresponding work hour preferences (Drago et. al, 2009). However there were mismatches that occurred for events such as mourning periods, reduced hours when children arrived, and flexible retirement options (Drago et. al, 2009). There were a variety of subjective factors, acknowledged by the authors of the study, which came into play in this research. However, it might also be suggested that this points to the conclusion that people want to work where they want to work based on what is happening in their lives.

If this is true, it makes sense to accommodate people and the motivation of the employer and employee could be aligned long term if this were the case.

A possible rebuttal statement you could make might be:

"But you can't accommodate everyone and some people may have unrealistic requests. If I allow an exception, then everyone will want it."

A possible rationale and approach could be as follows:

The response above is a common one, and probably untrue. The best way to find out would be to try. There are entire business models based on giving people the latitude to "do whatever they want", and it works out quite well, for example allowing people to pay whatever they want at a restaurant or working whatever hours they want to get a job done.

An example is cited in the Harvard Business Review (2012) by Riener & Traxler, who conducted a two year observation where only 0.5% of patrons at a restaurant took the opportunity to pay nothing, and get their food for free. The prices of meals had stabilized at a level that was above costs, and customers had increased by 50% due to the new practice (Harvard Business Review, 2012).

Kim et al. (2009) compares this pay what you want idea with, name your own price, as in an auction for example. The difference being that the seller can name a minimum price. They also give the example of the band Radiohead releasing its album online and allowing people to pay what they wanted for it. The album was downloaded 2 million times and the band reported that the format was profitable (Kim et al., 2009).

This doesn't always work, particularly with high priced products as there is a greater incentive to pay less (Kim et al., 2009). Kim et al. (2009) also cite things such as reference pricing, past prices paid, fairness, altruism, loyalty, price consciousness, income and satisfaction as factors that come into play in terms of what people are willing to pay for a product or service.

Here is another example:

In classes that I teach I tell the students that I don't care if they use their cell phones, they just can't bother the person next to them. I let them know if it's quiet go ahead, if they need to take a call, go outside. Guess how many people take them out and use them? The answer is very few and often times no one does.

A rebuttal statement might be:

"If you let it slide then people will start to take advantage."

Think about what that means, if you allow people to do what they want, they will do it? Why is that such a bad thing? Because it will negatively impact the business? Think about how so, and will the positive impact of empowering people and trusting them to make good decisions be more profitable in the long run, compared to exerting narrowly defined and often arbitrary rules on them about how to do their work?

Let's consider this, a situation where a customer shows up late to an appointment to have the oil changed on their car.

Employee to customer: "my manager would like to have a word with you, please."

Manager to customer: "this is the third time this year that you have showed up late to your appointment. I will be documenting this and if it happens again you will no longer be able to come here for an oil change."

Sounds stupid doesn't it. Now some businesses operate this way, think of the Soup Nazi from Seinfeld (it's worth looking up if you don't get the reference). Services that are high in demand can pick and choose their customers, they can provide poor service and it doesn't matter, people will keep coming in because there is a demand for the product or service and a lack of comparative supply. If some people choose to leave it's not enough incentive for the business to change its ways.

I would have you consider two things; the first is, do you think this is a good long term sustainable strategy with which to run your businesses? Secondly, is this how you want to run your business period? In both cases, likely not.

It should be the motivation of the employer to empower their employees and allow them latitude to do the job as they see fit, in order to better accommodate both employee and customer needs.

This is more complex than presented here, where we address this issue on the surface. We also have to consider switching costs, supply and demand of the product or service, available substitutes, etc. I suppose the main thing to consider is, is it a long term sustainable solution to lecture your customers? Probably not. Is it a long term sustainable solution to lecture your employees? Probably not.

I think of another everyday example, going to the dentist and having the hygienist lecture you about flossing (maybe not you but it happens to me). It doesn't make me want to floss, it makes we want to find someone who won't give me the lecture, I already know I don't floss.

Particular industries will provide various scenarios that influence employer motivations as well. Spears (2011) writes that even low price providers can benefit from an investment in employee training by focusing on models that leverage low employee turnover and high employee training and empowerment.

Spears (2011) gives the example of Wal-Mart in an economic crises reducing its product offering in order to get a cost reduction. But sales decreased because employees were not educated enough about what they were selling. An example that focuses on fewer products and higher levels of employee training and low turnover would be Costco and Trader Joe's (Spears, 2011).

Is it really the motivation of employers to get the most out of their employees for the least, or is it about getting the highest quality products and services to market? An employee service orientation would allow for both.

CHAPTER 5

Customer Motivation

"The early bird gets the worm, but the second mouse gets the cheese."

- Variously Ascribed

Now we will move our discussion deep into the mind of the customer.

What motivates customers? Is it the lowest price, quality products, superior customer service?

Likely all of the above, and it is also likely they are motivated by their own self-interest, and I mean that in a positive sense. Customers want to have their needs met, and get the goods, services, and experience that they are seeking.

It is a good exercise to consider the above premise of self-interest when looking at something like customer complaints. It is also a good exercise to consider positive intent on the part of the customer.

It is good practice to always assume positive intent. A good example is to think of anytime you went into a store, or went to see a professional service provider, and had a complaint about something. How did you feel if you were brushed off or not taken seriously? In my experience everyone has a legitimate complaint, and the key to that is to include "in their own mind", as a caveat. We will discuss some of this idea in the Self Awareness section later in the book.

Yes, there are customers that have mal intent, but this is the case with everything in life. Those exceptions need to be identified and dealt with in the appropriate manner. For the most part I would suggest that most people do what they do for a legitimate reason (again, one that they perceive to be legitimate).

Customers can also be used as a source of motivation for employees. Grant (2011), writes that customers can motivate employees more than managers can. He gives several examples such as banks bringing in customers that have been saved from debt by low interest loans. Or Facebook flying in users to meet with engineers and talks with them about how Facebook helped them to connect with family and friends (Grant, 2011). The article makes a good point, and cites several examples of where to look for these connections from employee to end user. Grant (2011) also acknowledges that employees will connect with end users differently, but that those employees that most need motivating are the ones whose connections with end users have the greatest impact.

I would also suggest that intuitively this idea makes sense, for example that people gain more satisfaction from satisfying a customer than by satisfying a manager. This may or may not be true depending on the self-interest of the individual employee. From what we will have discussed in this book about different motivational theories I would suggest that a majority of people are striving to provide work of value, not working simply to impress the boss.

And what does the customer get from all of this? Customers, the same as employees, are all different and have different motivations and expectations for interacting with businesses and employees.

Coget (2011) talks about how some of the factors that would induce customer motivation start at the management level. This is intuitive as what the organization's management chooses to implement and support will have a direct impact on a customer's motivation to return to that business.

Coget (2011) writes about Vroom's Contingency Theory, which

suggests that the motivation to perform a particular task or use a new technology is based on a person believing that effort will lead to performance, performance will result in positive outcomes, and that the outcomes are of a desired importance.

Think about this model in terms of having customers utilize a new technology such as self-scanning checkout machines. Do I believe I can use this new process? If I try will it be a better way to checkout and will I see added value in my shopping experience?

The ability for management to create a situation where employees are able to create a successful situation for customers is important in this case. Really in all cases it is important when it comes to new processes, or even maintaining old ones in times of continuous change in the competitive environment.

Think about how this would best happen in your operation. Would it be by management dictating the process, or employees being involved and able to give feedback and make decisions on the spot?

Think about what's next for your business, emerging technologies such as mobile purchases, increasing online purchases, increasingly convenient point of sale processes and enterprise management systems.

Coget (2011) writes that for a variety of reasons that charismatic managers (being that they have qualities that are expressive and engaging) are in a better position to have their motivation spill over to their subordinates, and are more likely to positively impact customer motivation.

The idea behind identifying and addressing customer motivation is to think about how your employees can assist your customers and deal with complaints. Are they empowered to do both?

Let's use the example of a service technician going to someone's house. What does good customer service look like? Do they engage in conversation with the customer? Or simply put their head down and get the job done as quickly and efficiently as possible?

It depends on the customer. Some people like having a conversation with someone they have brought into their home, and some people just want the job done and over with. Catering to that individual customer's need is good customer service. If the organization's policy, or its employees are trained to behave in a narrowly defined scope of practice, they lose the ability to adapt to their surroundings.

Companies could also start thinking bigger picture on this issue of customer service and customer motivation. For example, is it the amount of dollars per labor hour generated that's important or would focusing on dollars generated per the lifetime of a customer be a better way of looking at it?

People go to McDonalds for familiarity; for example you can get a Big Mac that tastes like a Big Mac almost anywhere in the world. Crane (2003) discusses McDonalds and new marketing strategies, suggesting that a throwback to advertising of the past may be a good way to reconnect with consumers. What has worked for your organization in the past? Is it worth revisiting old strategies? It can also be beneficial to look back and see why certain things were successful.

Rigby and Ledingham (2004) discuss some ways that you can become familiar with customers, through Customer Relationship Management Systems (CRMs). Essentially these systems manage customer data and pair it with company data to manage the entire customer relationship cycle from Targeting and Marketing, to Development of Offering, Sales, Superior Experience, Retention and Win Back, and then back again through the cycle (Rigby & Ledingham, 2004).

These systems are expensive and can result in large amounts of data, but the possibility of not gaining any knowledge or at least relevant knowledge, remains high.

Think about these things within the context of employee service. Marketing and customer relationship management typically get an external focus, but what about applying some of these concepts internally?

As we move towards a knowledge based economy, where differentiation is a source of competitive advantage, how does your business become the type of business that can develop familiarity with your customers?

Imagine a customer that is able to call their plumber and get the same type of service or even the same technician each time they need them. Trust is built, they know the type of experience they will have, and the employee knows as well. A lifelong relationship could be built meeting the needs of the customer, the employee, and the organization. How can you replicate this idea in your business?

Chapter 6

Self-Awareness

"The only way to do great work is to love what you do."

- Steve Jobs

Dale Carnegie (1936) wrote the famous book *How to Win Friends and Influence People*. If you haven't read it you should, but what stuck with me was the ideas that he presents around people and their own self-perception.

For example, Carnegie cites Al Capone, describing himself as a good person that was just misunderstood.

Everyone does this to some extent of course, but the reverse of it is not fully understanding, or not trying to understand another person's mindset. For example you're cut off in traffic, and upset at the other person being inconsiderate, maybe failing to consider the other person is rushing to a horrible emergency. If an employee is sick, are you upset you have to replace the shift, or assuming positive intent, and hoping they get well soon?

To catch these thoughts and feelings as they are going by can be difficult, especially in the heat of the moment or if you have a lot on your mind.

Being self aware helps to address some of the banal platitudes that we discussed earlier. We all agree that good communication is important, everyone nods, but what does that mean to you, specifically what does that entail? Do you have a hard time understanding why people don't just "pick up the phone", or why certain people can't be bothered to check their email?

Think about it and think about what is possible in these circumstances by asking others their opinion in an open and non-confrontational way. It can help you learn about others and their opinions, and likely more about yourself in the process.

There are also many ways that you can go about trying to investigate your own level of self-awareness through personality profiling. Myers Briggs, Insights Colors, DISC, True Colors, are some of the more well know tools used by organizations and consultants alike to help people better understand their own "personality profile".

Some positives from the sessions that I have facilitated are that it seems to be that 90% of the participants find these tool to be accurate in terms of the classification of their personality traits. It is suggested that if people are going through major life changes, or maybe addressing the tools from an "at home" perspective as opposed to a "work" perspective that this can also affect the results.

A downside to this type of personality profiling is that it can have the effect of pigeonholing people into very narrowly defined categories of a certain personality trait. For example:

"You behave this way because you are in the _____ personality category."

Self-awareness is an important concept to consider and work towards a fuller understanding of why people do what they do, and a further investigation of who is "right" and why.

I have spoken to a number of psychologists about personality profiling tools and they provided me with an interesting perspective. For example, consider that people fill out questions and then receive a report. They filled out the questions, so when they are surprised how accurate the tool is, they were the ones that filled out the questions. Who else would the report be describing?

Self-awareness is effective from all vantage points of your business.

There are many employees that want to be in charge or think they can do things better than their supervisor. But they soon find out why things were done the way they were done once they get to that position. The same could likely be said of managers inferring what they know about the roles of their employees in the operation.

When managers make assumptions about how employees are spending their time, are they assuming positive intent?
Is that employee, manager, customer, business really lazy and incompetent, or are there reasons for it that you may be forced to deal with if you were placed in a similar position?

CHAPTER 7

The Customer is Always Right

"You can't help respecting anybody who can spell Tuesday, even if they don't spell it right; but spelling isn't everything. There are days when spelling Tuesday simply doesn't count"

- Winnie The Pooh

Here are some quotes attributed to customer service that would also apply to the concept of employee service.

The quotes are compared to how their meaning could apply to employee service, and show how it can make just as much business sense to say that the employee is always right.

"Your most unhappy customers are your greatest source of learning." - Bill Gates

If you are not listening to your employees you are missing an opportunity. The trouble with listening to your employees is that you run the risk of soliciting opinions, only to have to make a decision and it's hard (impossible) to please everyone. The truth is that involving more people and more opinions gives you a different perspective and results in higher quality decision making.

The other consideration around this idea is that in general, people only tend to give feedback when they are very happy or very dissatisfied. For example, changing a process or product for one dissatisfied customer or employee may also discount the majority of others that are benefitting from the current system, product, or procedure already in place.

It seems there needs to be a balance between being open to feedback and having adequate mechanisms in place to solicit this feedback. It is also important to take feedback "with a grain of salt", or be able to look at opinions and feedback in the broader context.

It is also important to consider for both customers and employees, that things become corrected before that person becomes "your most unhappy customer or employee". Again it may be difficult for the employee to voice this feedback if there is not an adequate mechanism in place to do so. And it would be unfortunate if the only tool available to address feedback of unhappy employees is an exit interview, because by that time it's usually too late.

"It is not the employer who pays the wages. Employers only handle the money. It is the customer who pays the wages."
- Henry Ford

Employees make the money, they pay the bills, by serving the customer. It's an interesting perspective when employees realize that great customer service is in their best interest. Similarly when employers see that great treatment of employees and catering to their needs, is in their best interest as well.

It can be overly simplistic to suggest that one group is more responsible for the success of the organization than another. The truth is that everyone works together and creates the environment for success.

Remember that as with anything else, there are a small percentage of customers that are not good for a business. I have heard many stories and encountered it myself, where customers are turned away because they are abusive, irrational, overly demanding of the resources or staff of the businesses. The same can be said of employees, managers, or products; certain ones you don't want around but in general the majority work together to create successful opportunities for all stakeholders.

I have several examples where support services employees have told me that they are a lower priority employee because it is the field employees that do the work and are making the money. I typically explain another perspective that without, for example, accounts payable paying the bills and sending out paychecks, none of that work would be done. Also reinforcing that these kinds of support services are an equally important "cog in the machine", and equally responsible for an organizations success is key.

"Spend a lot of time talking to customers face to face. You'd be amazed how many companies don't listen to their customers." -Ross Perot

I think you would be equally amazed how many companies don't talk face to face with their employees, or how many organizations make unilateral decisions without consulting front line workers.

Organizations have more customers or end users than they do employees. So why is it that we always hear about companies listening to their customers, and not employees?

Again you have to find the balance between listening to everyone and then having to make a decision that does not necessarily please everyone. But there is no reason to do this for customers and not employees. Employees may have more insight into what the customers want than the customers do. For example think of the famous Henry Ford quote "if I asked people what they wanted they would have said faster horses".

"If you do build a great experience, customers tell each other about that. Word of mouth is very powerful."
- Jeff Bezos

Employees will also tell others about their experience and whether it was good or bad. Have you ever heard a story about someone's bad boss, or how the company "screwed them over"? Probably at least once and if it hasn't happened to you or you haven't heard of an example, I think you are in the minority.

Word of mouth travels equally fast for an employer that is terrible to work for, or is managing the business in a way that employees may have a negative view of.

It is important to consider employee word of mouth as well, because they spend more time with the organization than a customer does. This means more opportunity to see all of the good and the bad that an organization is representative of.

"The customer experience is the next competitive battleground." - Jerry Gregoire

It could also be said that the employee experience is the next competitive battleground. Companies such as Google are hailed as the greatest places to work and are making efforts towards the employee experience for a reason. It could be viewed almost as a chicken and egg situation; can Google offer what it does to its employees because of its success, or is the company successful because of what it has done for its employees. Maybe it's a little bit of both. Google is the world's first brand to be valued at a billion dollars (Manimala & Wasdani, 2013).

Based on the approach of this book it could be argued that a great employee experience is a strong predictor, or necessary component, to a great customer experience.

"Customer satisfaction is worthless. Customer loyalty is priceless." - Jeffrey Gitomer

Think about what a lifetime employee is worth to an organization. The knowledge, expertise, skills, and loyalty that can be developed and retained is likely not quantifiable, but likely valuable.

Would you sell to a customer planning only to sell to them for a year or two, thinking they will move to a competitor? Why would you approach the employment relationship any differently? Does the customer have a say in terms of how long you sell to them? Should the employee have a similar say in terms of how long they work for an organization?

If an employee is satisfied I wouldn't say that is worth nothing necessarily, but employee loyalty is worth far more. What if you could have both - a loyal and satisfied employee?

I think a good example is employees that wear their company jackets out in public places. People will ask them what they do and they will say they work for your business, and hopefully that it's a great place to work.

This is advertising, promotion, and could be employee recruitment, and if people like telling others where they work it could be a source of retention.

"Quality in a service or product is not what you put into it. It is what the client or customer gets out of it." - Peter Drucker

The question you should ask yourself is, do you believe that more satisfied employees create products and services that customers are more likely to get an increased value out of? Or at least more than what an unsatisfied employee would be able to provide?

As the North American economy shifts from that of manufacturing to a more service based economy, intangible components of products and services become a greater source of competitive advantage. These intangibles are created and distributed by employees and are subjective and difficult to measure.

Put what you want into your employee training, it only matters what they are getting out of it so that they can they serve customers and become an asset to the organization.

You could also say that a company could put whatever they want into a product or service, if an employee is not positioned to help the customer get the most value out of that product or service, this is a disparity that will have a negative impact on the business, the customer, and likely the employee as well.

"Customers don't expect you to be perfect. They do expect you to fix things when they go wrong." - Donald Porter

The same comment could be attributed to employees. If equipment is broken, if a process does not make sense, employees expect (and rightly so) that the organization will fix the problems. Failure to do so may result in unhappy employees, lower quality outputs, and dissatisfied customers.

A central issue here is empowering employees and supervisors to fix problems. When a situation occurs and an employee has to fill out a form and submit to his or her supervisor to then forward to a Vice President, to fix an issue that could have been solved within the timeframe of the paperwork, this creates an unnecessary bottleneck.

Bottleneck processes like this have likely been developed as a solution to mitigate abuse of funds or authority or whatever has been an issue for an organization in the past. Again I would ask, is a process that wastes time and money, every time, worth the savings of dollars that would have happened in a case of "authority abuse" in a minority of situations?

When things go wrong it is important that managers, employees, and even customers can be empowered to fix problems.

"There is a spiritual aspect to our lives – when we give we receive – when a business does something good for somebody, that somebody feels good about them!"- Ben Cohen

Phrased similarly, when an organization does something good for an employee, the employee feels good about the organization. This concept of reciprocity exists for employees as well as customers. Customers want to keep coming back to the organization that meets their needs, and is a positive force in their lives. Employees as well want to keep coming back to an organization that does good things for them, and they are more likely to do good things for the organization.

"The more you engage with customers the clearer things become and the easier it is to determine what you should be doing." - John Russell

I might suggest that the rationale behind this quote is that the better you can understand your customer, the better you will understand what you need to do to meet their needs.

The same can be said for employees, if you do not know them on a personal and professional level, how can you know what to provide to them in order to create the environment necessary for mutual success?

How to do this is the harder questions, and there is no one size fits all approach for an organization. However, hopefully some of the questions asked and answered in this book will help lead you to the correct processes for effective engagement with your employees.

"Being on par in terms of price and quality only gets you into the game. Service wins the game." - Tony Allesandra

You can hire an employee for a job with pay and benefits but it will be the intangible things that keep them around. For example, if they need an extra day bereavement leave, can they have it? If they want it everyone will want it. Is that true, and what would the consequences be?

In Andrew DuBrin's (2003) book Winning at Office Politics he talks about it being ridiculous that an employee would fudge an expense report, to possibly gain a few hundred dollars when, if caught, could lose their job.

I believe this is analogous to digging your heals in for an extra days pay for bereavement leave at the risk of upsetting that employee and have them starting to look for other work. You likely have bigger fish to fry.

I also don't believe that it will "open the flood gates" either. Some people will abuse the system, but most won't and it's not worth upsetting the majority because of the misguided actions of the few (of which they likely have a rationalization in their own mind for their behavior).

You have to make these judgment calls, but I would suggest that the majority of the time it is important to have an "employee service" orientation towards employee wants and needs.

"In the world of Internet Customer Service, it's important to remember your competitor is only one mouse click away."
- Doug Warner

The new age of social media and platforms such as LinkedIn provide your employees with a very convenient way to look for other places to ply their trade.

With the explosion of mobile technology they can even do it on their phone on their coffee break. While working for you they could be networking and finding better places to work for more money, better benefits, with people that are already in their social network.

"Make your product easier to buy than your competition, or you will find your customers buying from them, not you."
- Mark Cuban

How easy is it for an employee to apply for a job or talk to someone about an opportunity at your organization?

Do you think that a highly qualified and sought after employee will attempt to navigate your user unfriendly HR automated application portal?

It should be an easy process. Many companies put their "career opportunities" link right on the front page of their website. There are many companies that talk about how difficult it is to get qualified employees, but how much effort do they put into making it easy for these people to apply?

Do customers simply show up at your doorstep when you open for business, or do you have to advertise and engage in sales and marketing efforts? Why would it be so much different for employees?

I also find it astonishing the number of companies that will not call unsuccessful candidates after an interview. Likely the same people that get upset when people change jobs and give no notice. Maybe that person was unsuccessful, but you shortlisted them and they may likely be a good fit for something in the future.

They might tell a few people how surprised they were that you actually took the time and courtesy to call them and discuss how the interview went.

"If you work just for money, you'll never make it, but if you love what you're doing and you always put the customer first, success will be yours." - Ray Krock

If you love what you do and the people you do it with, by putting those employees first, your chances of success will be higher.

Numerous hiring managers tell me that many times they are hiring the person, as much or more so, than they are hiring their qualifications. The rationale given is that the job itself will likely change due to the increasingly accelerated pace of technology change and globalization, so it is more important for an employee to have some of the more adaptive soft skills rather than hard technical skills of a particular process or technology in order to be successful.

Many of those components will center around employee satisfaction, which can only be attained by maintaining an employee service attitude towards attraction and retention of employees.

"We see our customers as invited guests to a party, and we are the hosts. It's our job every day to make every important aspect of the customer experience a little bit better." - Jeff Bezos

Employees are really your invited guests as well, they don't have to stay. They can be people that are enjoying the party and contributing to the fun and excitement, or not having a good time and sitting in the corner. A lot of that has to do with the host (the organization), and the environment that they create for the people at "the party".

What do you or your organization do to make the employee experience a little bit better?

"Don't try to tell the customer what he wants. If you want to be smart, be smart in the shower. Then get out, go to work and serve the customer!" - Gene Buckley

You can try to tell an employee what they want, or what is good for them, but a superior strategy is to find out what they want and cater to their needs.

Think of examples from your own life about an experience you have had with a paternalistic or micro-managing supervisor. How did it feel when they told you when you should take your vacation or how you should feel about, or perform your job duties?

"Every company's greatest assets are its customers, because without customers there is no company." - Michael LeBoeuf

I believe that a good argument exists, that a company's greatest assets are its employees. Remember that without employees there is also no company. Or if you are unable to attract and retain the highest quality of employees your competitive advantage will suffer.

At the very least, you're leaving something on the table if you are not considering the "asset value" of your employees as your most important.

"It helps a ton when you learn people's names and don't butcher them when trying to pronounce them." - Jerry Yang

I had once thought that being able to remember people's names was a somewhat arbitrary skill until an example that was put to me by someone that had a difficult name to pronounce.

This person mentioned that when her name was pronounced correctly that she could see that the individual had taken the time to learn her name and pronounce it correctly, and that made her feel valued.

"Our mission statement about treating people with respect and dignity is not just words but a creed we live by every day. You can't expect your employees to exceed the expectations of your customers if you don't exceed the employees' expectations of management." - Howard Schultz

How do you exceed your employees' expectations of the organization and its management?

It is more difficult than the quote sounds, as people have very different expectations about the type of treatment that they "should" be receiving at work.

I have heard some managers and business owners refer to it as a sense of entitlement by employees, in terms of employees expecting certain behaviors or tangible items from management.

I might counter this idea of entitlement by illustrating the fact that the idea of "retirement" from work is relatively new. For the majority of human history, people worked until they were dead. The idea that people want "more", or to find ways to make their life easier seems to be a component of the human condition, and one that seems to have had an overall positive effect on the long term quality of life for everyone.

So when looking at the idea that an employee "expects" certain things, it might be important to consider their perspective, or what it might mean to them should you be able to provide it.

There are some caveats here that we will address elsewhere in the book.

"The customer's perception is your reality." - Kate Zabriskie

The employee's perception becomes the organization's reality. For example if employees perceive that the organization has "short changed" them, they may react accordingly.

If employees feel that they are valued and are empowered to do valuable work, they will react accordingly.

If your organization is able to create an environment where employees perceive that they are empowered to make decisions and help customers and the organization, that will become the reality as well.

"Every client you keep, is one less that you need to find."
- Nigel Sanders

In fact this quote applies to employees as well. Now clearly you want to ensure that you are keeping the right people for the right reasons, but you don't want to have to find new people because of the wrong reasons.

"You are serving a customer, not a life sentence. Learn how to enjoy your work." - Laurie McIntosh

Learn how to help your employees enjoy their work. Yes you are paying them to do a job, but it will be a far better relationship and outcome, if you create an environment where that employee will enjoy coming to work day after day, and not feeling like that are serving "a life sentence".

"It starts with respect. If you respect the customer as a human being, and truly honor their right to be treated fairly and honestly, everything else is much easier." - Doug Smith

At the end of the day, as per our Chapter 1 quote, you usually get the employees that you deserve which is likely true related to employees and respect. You get what you give.

Chapter 8

Employee Attraction and Retention

"When people are financially invested, they want a return. When people are emotionally invested, they want to contribute."

- Simon Sinek

Many of the supervisors and company owners that I work with tell me, and you have probably heard or said it yourself, "good employees are hard to find". Could it also be the case that good employers are hard to find?

Employee turnover is a major issue for a business - do you track yours?

The formula looks like this:

T = Employee Turnover
X = Employees that left the organization during that period
B = Number of employees at the beginning of the period
E = Number of employees at the end of the period

$$T = X / ((B-E)/2)$$

This translates essentially to the number of employees that left divided by the average number of employees that you had during the time period that you're looking at, whether that's quarter, year, five years etc.

I remember teaching a management course and discussing employee turnover and one of the attendees gave an interesting perspective. He cited that he was not concerned about the turnover of low wage entry level employees, that he expected those positions to turn over. He was more concerned with the turnover of higher experienced, higher level employees. My first thought for example was, how do you intend to replace those high level employees without developing entry level employees to fill those positions? In fact, he expected them to leave the company.

Employees want to work for the best employers. That means a number of things, and likely different things to different people.

In his January 13, 2014 speaker series at the Red Deer Chamber of Commerce, Brian Burke was at the time the president of hockey operation for the Calgary Flames hockey team in Alberta, Canada. He suggested that in addition to high taxes, getting new facilities in Canada was another barrier to attracting those employees (players) to work in the Canadian marketplace, as the players like those things.

The points that he made were really about hockey players being human beings and they want and respond to different things. Some players like to play in Florida, where they are relative unknowns and there is no state tax. Some love the public eye and want to play in big markets where they are celebrities.

Think about your motivations at work - do you like a new office space to work in, new equipment, the latest software, would you like to pay lower taxes?

Do some of your employees like the social aspect of work, and do some like keeping to themselves?

Keep these things in mind, and also consider that many times it is not a preference for people, it is the way they are and how they naturally tend to behave.

I remember speaking with someone that was very grateful that the instructor for one of the courses she was taking was considerate of her anxiety disorder and not putting her on the spot or singling her out in front of a classroom. I might suggest people have similar needs in the workplace, which they are not requesting by choice, but that they need to have accommodated to function. And maybe they don't feel overly comfortable disclosing all the details to their employer. Is that ok? In what situation would that not be ok and the condition would need to be disclosed?

Fulmer, Gerhant & Scott (2003) conducted an interesting study on whether or not the organizations that were ranked in the 100 best places to work, were in fact better performers than their counterparts within the same industry. Their conclusions supported their hypothesis in that yes, the top 100 ranked companies had employees that had positive attitudes and the employees remained with the organization over time. They also concluded that accounting ratios were generally better for the top 100 than for others. It was also concluded that at minimum these organizations are able to create great workplaces without hurting the bottom line, and it many cases they exhibit superior performance (Fulmer et. al, 2003).

I don't believe you will ever find a company that would claim to be a poor place to work, or at least that they are creating that environment intentionally.

For example, look at some job advertisements. Most will say things like:

- Opportunities for advancement
- Career training
- Flexible hours
- Great benefits
- Competitive wages

You probably won't see:

- Discouraged to stay home when you are sick
- Will need to ask for raise
- New employees will be hired at the same wage as senior employees
- If you start working here and don't like it, you can leave

The first rule of sales is to under promise and over deliver. You are selling your new employee on wanting to work at your organization. You want them there not just for 6 months, hopefully 6 years and maybe 60 years.

If you manage to "trick" someone into working for you with promises of a great work-life balance and then pressure them to work all the time, it won't last long. Think of some examples from your own life. How does it feel to be overpromised and under-delivered to?

CHAPTER 9

Marketing and Branding

"Timid salespeople have skinny kids."

– Zig Ziglar

When your customers need the product or service that you offer, you want them to think of your company when they need it.

Imagine if you could create the same situation for attracting employees. For example, a plumber leaves school and says, "I want to work for company Y, they seem like a great organization to work for".

There are many organizations that have this type of branding as organizations that are "employee friendly". Google, General Electric, Drop Box etc. Are there any other organizations you can think of? What makes this so?

Wilkinson et al. (2014) compiled a list of the best places to work in IT in 2014. Some things included in the reasons why certain organizations made the list included:

- Candy counter
- Basketball court
- Pool table
- 200 hours of technical training and mentorship program
- Child care facilities
- Starbucks coffee shops
- Social networks and commitment to corporate culture and goals
- Lactation rooms
- Standing desks, yoga rooms, fresh fruit

- Telecommuting options

The list could go on and on as companies are attempting new ways to be viewed as employee friendly in an attempt to attract and retain top talent.

Priyadarshi (2011) conducted a study of Indian companies to determine the correlation between employer brand image and it's relation to job satisfaction, commitment, and turnover. The results of the study were mixed, but it was found that an employee's perception of the companies brand image was shaped by a variety of personal and professional experiences, which ultimately shaped their attitudes towards the company (Priyadarshi, 2011). Regression models were run on the data and only organizational structure and flexibility were found to be directly related to job satisfaction, commitment and turnover (Priyadarshi, 2011).

The study points to an important conclusion, that you can tell an employee what the company brand image is, but they are going to perceive it based on their own individual backgrounds and experiences. I think this makes intuitive sense as well and another example of where actions and the employee experience will mean more than the words and advertisements of the employer.

Does your organization spend more time telling employees what it is they are to perceive the company to be, or finding out how employees see the brand image?

If these things are true, it's not possible for an organization to disagree with an employee's perception of how they are experiencing their employment with the company. Their perception is their reality.

Let's look at some examples of contrasting opinions of what is considered employee friendly that could and do occur in a variety of workplaces:

- An organization permits smoking breaks, non-smoking employees feel they are being short changed because they do not take as many breaks because they do not smoke.

- People that live out of town are paid when they can't come into work because of severe weather. People that live out of town are thankful, and those that have to come into work feel it is unfair that just because people live out of town they get a day off with pay.

- People with children are allowed to attend their child's events and appointments. Great flexibility and autonomy for those workers, but what about those without children?

- A manager that gets their hair cut on company time feels that "it grows on company time, it gets cut on company time".

- A company likes to throw an extravagant Christmas party. People of other faiths or that do not celebrate Christmas may not feel this is fair as they do not receive a similar event.

- Employees get unlimited sick time, which is great for employees but employers, supervisors, and other employees may feel taken advantage of if they believe some individuals are "abusing the system". Some employees may think it's not fair if some people are "sick" more often than others. If that policy is ever taken away it will negatively affect those that never took sick time. Some people feel sick bank time is a part of their regular wage.

Wilden, Gudergan and Lings (2010) discusses employer branding in terms of the recruitment package of psychological, economic and functional benefits that employees associate being employed with a particular company. Wilden et al. (2010) concludes that employees are basing these perceptions on:

- Previous direct work experience with either the employer directly or in the sector.

- Clarity, credibility and consistency of the employer's

projection of the branding signals.

- Perceptions of the employer's brand investments.

- Perceptions of the employer's product or service brand portfolio.

Wilden et al. (2010) wrote an excellent paper that delves deep into the psychology of branding and how that relates to attraction and retention of employees.

To make a concise statement on the ideas in their paper, I would suggest that people want to work where they "perceive" they will have the best experience (based on their own personal values and what is important to them).

It could be suggested that the issue lies in the "truth behind the advertising" so to speak. For example, Amazon.com might have their own "brand" that they paid a marketing company a lot of money to develop. My own personal experience with them is that they are a brand of "excellent quality, convenience, and low cost". I don't know what their official branding statement is, and I don't care. I like dealing with them because of the high level of quality and service that they offer me.

If I was an employee I don't care what the marketing department developed and put on the wall, I care about how I am treated every day. I speak with many employees that are unaware of what the Vision, Mission, or Value statements of their company are. When asked why, a typical answer is that they do not identify with it or it is not communicated enough within the organization.

Try having your employees write what they think the Mission, Vision, and Values of the company should be based on - their experience - or to have customers complete the same exercise and see what they come up with. If they all align with each other that is probably a good indication that an organization is on the right track in terms of branding. If they differ to a significant degree than the branding and communication of the organization's Mission, Vision, and Values needs to be revisited.

Let's look again at the idea that no company is going to say they don't value employees as per the following example:

I was consulting at a large multi-national company and met a newly hired HR and Marketing department team that was going to design and market employee training to suit the needs of the organization and its employees. There was a discussion about the organizational culture around training and the culture in general.

The question that I had thought of after the fact was, how could it be a possible that they had an in depth knowledge of the organizational culture if none of the employees on the team had been working at the organization for more a year?

Yes they could "ask around" but that would get a limited perspective. A marketing company that is possibly located in another country could come up with the marketing campaign to attract workers. Most of them are very similar, including many of the platitudes and clichés that we have discussed earlier.

Is this a negative thing?

It's only negative if the gap between what is being advertised and what is being experienced affects the employees experience or "brand perception" of the employer.

Many of us likely do not exhibit a large degree of "buyer's remorse" when we drink a sports drink and find we still can't play basketball like Michael Jordan. However, it would be quite a letdown to be told you will get a certain wage to find out that you don't, or certain benefits and you don't, or that you and your opinion and contribution are valued and they aren't.

Some of these things relate to employment contracts in writing, or implied obligations of employees or employers, but a lot of it has to do with an emotional contract formed by the two parties.

Is an emotional contract enforceable?

Beltrami (2011) discusses platitudes in marketing and writes a call to action in moving towards more principal based marketing and advertising. You could argue the same not only for your products and services, but as an employer or an organization as a whole, and that this is an important concept and component of success.

Beltrami (2011) cites items such as hair splitting claims with minimal disclosure, emotional manipulation, and a lack of committed attitude to use ethical advertising. The same can be said for employer branding.

Do some of these things apply to how you attract and retain employees?

Sirianni et al. (2013) wrote that although branding can enable marketers to add symbolic meaning, it is ultimately the end customer that determines what a brand means to them.

What does your organizational brand mean to your employees as an employer? Have you ever asked them, and if not, why not?

Sirianni et al. (2013) also states that there are many brand encounters that are not regularly managed as part of the brands position strategy, for example, between front line employees and customers.

I might also suggest that the brand encounters between employees and the organization as an employer is a brand position that is also not regularly managed by many companies.

Cialdini (1993) as cited in Sirianni et al. (2013) state that research has shown that every person to person communication is often more persuasive than other forms of advertising.

Think about that statement in terms of what your organization does when marketing and advertising for recruitment, attraction, and retention of employees. How much of your person to person communication still exists in the age of increased electronic communications?

Think also about the idea of aligning an employee's behavior with what you believe the organizational brand to be. In terms of front line to customer personal interaction, would this be easier if the employee was treated as well as the customer, or if they are treated far worse or far better?

I might suggest that at least an equal treatment, from a brand perspective, would help to create an environment of competitive advantage.

Sirianni et al. (2013) propose that when employee behavior is aligned with the organizations brand, that this helps to link the employee and the brand in the customers' knowledge structure. In other words that the employee will represent the organization and brand and the customer will recognize this.

Sirianni et al. (2013) cite that front line employees are an important source of brand information and a key component in an organizations brand building strategy, in order to deliver the brands image.

Suppose your organizations brand is one of friendly, knowledgeable, and high quality service. If employees are not treated in a friendly way, not given proper training and opportunities for professional development, and not put as an organizational priority, is it easier or more difficult for employees to be put in a position of success to deliver this brand image to the customer?

CHAPTER 10

Change Management

"Change will not come if we wait for some other person or some other time. We are the ones we've been waiting for. We are the change that we seek."

-Barak Obama

In order to implement the changes required for your organization to move towards a higher degree of employee service through employee empowerment, change management processes will have to be implemented. We will look first at what employee empowerment is and then how to get there.

Ghosh (2013) presents this idea in that employee empowerment should be used as a strategic tool to obtain competitive advantage, and that there are some additional factors to consider.

We will look at these factors in this chapter, and then come up with a change management approach that will help you work towards a high level of employee empowerment and employee service within your organization.

Ghosh (2013) provides the definition of employee empowerment as an employee that has worked to develop their knowledge, skill, and ability over the job. If they are given overall charge over the work they do with adequate authority and responsibility, they can make decisions on their own and efficiently and effectively accomplish the job. It is the expectation of most people that they should have the power, authority, recognition, status, and responsibility. When they get these things they will be able to utilize their full potential, energy, abilities, and competence in an attempt to enhance their performance (Ghosh, 2013).

There are also different perspectives of empowerment as put forth by Ghosh (2013):

Social Perspective – to effectively empower employees from the social perspective, it is important to give appropriate authority and responsibility to middle managers so they can create an environment that meets employee social needs (Ghosh, 2013).

Psychological Perspective – people desire status, recognition, authority, responsibility, and challenging work with opportunities for advancement (Ghosh, 2013). Employees can therefore give their best and contribute to the goals of the organization if there esteem needs are met (Ghosh, 2013).

Growth Perspective – even when people have strong technical skills, they also need power, authority, and autonomy in decision making in order to reach their peak performance (Ghosh, 2013).

Organizational Perspective – because employee empowerment is a source of competitive advantage by being able to provide added value to goods and services, these things must be provided by committed, competent, and loyal employees which can be accomplished through empowerment (Ghosh, 2013).

Approaching empowerment as a source of sustainable competitive advantage, Ghosh (2013) writes that sustainable competitive advantage is attainable through employee empowerment.

Barney (1991, 1995), as cited in Ghosh (2013) indicates that in order to produce sustainable competitive advantage a resource must:

1) Be valuable and create value for the organization

2) Be rare

3) Be difficult to imitate

4) Be utilized in an organization that has appropriate structures and systems in place that can effectively and efficiently utilize the resource.

Resources that contain these qualities and would be said to sustain competitive advantage are rare, but human resources are able to meet these criteria (Ghosh, 2013).

Noorzilla et al. (2006) as cited in Ghosh (2013) states that utilizing employee empowerment is one of the most powerful ways that human resources practices can facilitate the contribution of people. And that these people are capable of creating value in product and service areas that is rare and difficult to imitate.

Ghosh (2013) cites several factors that are critical components to the success of employee empowerment:

1) A spontaneous desire and acceptance of the empowerment initiative by both the supervisor and subordinate

2) The empowered employee must have a high degree of self efficacy with regards to the high level of responsibility assigned

3) Trust and openness must exist between the supervisor and subordinate and they must have a healthy dyadic relationship

4) The supervisor must express an attitude of sharing information, responsibility, and offering assistance for successful task completion

5) The employee must have a high level of commitment towards work and the organization

6) Honest efforts on the part of the organization to enhance the level of employee competence for executing their responsibilities.

Ghosh (2013) also cites several barriers that may hinder employee empowerment:

1) Contaminated ego state – ego patterns of both supervisors and employees can hinder employee empowerment. An example might be a paternalistic relationship between supervisor and employee.

2) Absence of urge for a job – if employees have accepted a job for something to do or to pass the time versus needing one to make a living, there may be less incentive to take on any extra responsibility or risk and to maintain the status quo.

3) Autocratic management approach – if the organization is run by close monitoring and control by supervisors, employees may be less likely to view management with credibility. This may result in mistrust of management and fear losing their jobs, which will create an environment where employees may be unwilling to take responsibility for their actions.

4) Power centric manager – if a supervisor has a desire to hold on to power there may be less of a willingness to shift some of that power and responsibility to immediate subordinates.

5) Lack of willingness, desire, and competence of employees – if the employee does not want, or is not capable of taking on authority or responsibility, it is unlikely that an organization will get results from an employee empowerment initiative.

6) Cumbersome process activities – for effective employee empowerment an organization must run through such processes as assessment of need, selection devices, hiring employees, promoting competence and commitment amongst employee etc. Many organizations may not be willing to undertake this process if the activities and investment in these processes is cumbersome.

7) Top management priority – the level of priority that employee empowerment is given directly relates to the success of the initiative. If top priority is given it is more likely the process will function smoothly, but conversely the initiative may not be as successful if top management does not see employee empowerment as high on the priority list.

8) Unhealthy industrial relations – if there is a negative perception or ill will amongst employees and management, then employee empowerment will likely be ineffective.

9) Organizational culture – the organizational culture will guide the employee empowerment process, in either a positive or negative manner depending on the culture present.

Ghosh (2013) outlines some processes to work towards a successful employee empowerment initiative:

1) Awareness development program – it is important to create an awareness program to communicate what employee empowerment is, to generate interest, desire, and willingness to accept the program.

2) Developing competencies of empowered employees – tailored training should be given to empowered employees to enhance both their technical and people skills in the workplace. This will help to promote relationships and high quality outputs.

3) Attitudes and style of supervisor – a supervisor's attitude towards subordinates should be positive, supportive, facilitating, helpful, and motivating to make them feel like they work in a comfortable environment that is conducive to an empowered employee environment.

4) Organizational culture – creating and sustaining a positive workplace culture that aligns with the organization's mission, vision, and values, and is conducive to employee

empowerment will help to foster this type of an initiative.

I have consistently found that organizations struggle with change management for reasons that have mainly to do with employee buy-in. Employee buy-in can be difficult because in the typical organization, vague goals are set with ambiguous or arbitrary timelines.

We discussed the use of SMART goals earlier, which stands for (there are variations):

- Specific

- Measurable

- Achievable

- Relevant

- Timely

Your goals need to be SPECIFIC. For example, I want to sell more product, I want to increase my communication skills, I want to lose weight, make more money etc. These goals are nothing unless you specify what you actually mean. For example my goal is to increase sales by 5% next year in the widget product line by expanding to the surrounding local market of city Y.

Your goals need to be MEASURABLE. For example you could measure the increase in sales in a quantitative way that would show improvement. Things such as increasing customer satisfaction can be more difficult to measure, as qualifying metrics are more difficult to measure in most cases.

Your goals need to be ACHIEVABLE. For example, is a 5% increase even reasonable based on similar situations elsewhere? Do you have the resources to do this?

Goals must be RELEVANT. For example, if you are trying to

increase sales in a discontinued product line, this is not a relevant goal for sustained operations.

Goals must be TIMELY. There must be a timeline associated with goals so that progress can be measured using this metric.

Now that we have some SMART goals we can integrate this with the employee buy-in side of Change Management.

Goal setting should include the input of all employees and stakeholders. In this way the initiative is not simply imposed on them. It is likely that additional employee empowerment and autonomy will be welcomed by most.

Looking at what employee empowerment is and thinking about what we have discussed in previous chapters, use the SMART goal framework to develop a change management plan to move towards an employee service and employee empowerment culture within your organization.

A sample plan might look like this:

Vague and ambiguous goal: Our goal is to move towards increased levels of employee empowerment and towards an employee service orientation as defined by Kurt Spady in "The Employee is Always Right".

SMART Goal

Specific: Within one calendar year the organization will reduce its rate of employee turnover by 10%.

Measurable: The organization will be able to track this initiative by setting benchmarks for the rates of employee turnover over the last 3 years.

Achievable: This rate is consistent with other organizations in the industry and the goal is achievable.

Relevant: The fact that employee turnover is a significant cost and source of competitive advantage for the company, this is a relevant goal.

Timely: This goal will be achieved by the end of the company's fiscal year.

Now that we have our goals it's important to get employee buy-in and have everyone working towards the goal of retaining employees through an empowerment initiative.

Combining the hard targets of percentages and timelines with the more qualitative aspects of the benefits of employee empowerment would be a good way to approach this.

The other thing to remember is that it does not matter so much that an idea is good; it matters more that the idea is communicated in such as way as to get people to believe in it and support it through action.

A good first step in the communication process is to involve key stakeholders in the process of goal development. Start by going to employees with the targets to see if they make sense and why, what can be done to ensure that the goals are SMART, and that the required resources are in place to achieve success.

Next would be to create a marketing, branding, and awareness campaign around the initiative and why the organization is pursuing it. It can be far more helpful to start with the Why, than to begin with the What people need to start doing, and How they are going to have to do it.

Now we come to the What and the How. People can be informed through Steering Committees or Working Groups (depending on the size of the organization) as to what needs to happen next, and how it needs to be approached.

Again the Why, What, and How is best approached by actively involving representatives from stakeholder groups in the process, and then proceeding with appropriate communication. In this way you can improve the chances that employees will buy in and that you will be able to better anticipate barriers to success.

Many change management initiatives fail, not because the idea was not good, but because the right people were not involved in the discussions up front, and an implementation plan was not communicated in an appropriate fashion.

It is also important that after the change process is completed that new employee empowerment initiatives are reinforced by showing that the changes are creating success within the organization.

CHAPTER 11

Unions and Collective Agreements

"Alone we can do so little, together we can do so much."

-Helen Keller

I felt it important to include a brief section on working with employees that belong to unions and working with collective agreements or other forms of restrictive employment contracts.

The argument against "the employee is always right" would be that there are situations where the employee is very much in the wrong, and union representation and/or collective agreements put barriers up for managing these employees effectively.

Do you agree?

I might also argue that maybe if management acknowledged that "the employee is always right", there would be less of a need for organized labor in the form of unionization.

I have also been a part of too many situations where an employee's needs would have been met if they were a member of the union. Because they are "out of scope" upper management simply will often choose not to deal their concerns because they don't have to, and often there is no mechanism for such an employee to address these concerns.

Have you ever witnessed this in your unionized workplace?

Union is a very emotionally charged term but I would have you consider this: is it possible that an abusive union is just as damaging as abusive management?

Goddard and Frege (2013) cite the decline in union representation and look to see if management imposed systems are being created to fill the gap. They conclude that much of their finding is based on employee perceptions and that unions still have an impact in the democratization of the authority relationship within an organization (Goddard & Frege, 2013). They also state that their findings indicate that union workers are more likely to distrust management and evaluate authority relationships less favorably than non-unionized workers would be (Goddard & Frege, 2013).

Much of the organized labor discussion is out of the scope of this book, but I would ask you to consider the following questions:

- Do you agree with the "if the employee doesn't like it they can leave" approach?

- Does this apply if the issue the employee has is a safety issue?

- Would you say that unions have been responsible for things such as higher wages and better benefits for workers?

- Do you feel that unions "protect poor performing employees"?

- Do you feel unionization is still "necessary" in today's working environment?

Some important things to think about if they apply to you or your organization. It's a complicated discussion with many variables and points of view. Your answers to some of these questions may help you to determine your stance on unions and organized labor in general, which is also an important part of the discussion.

Regardless of your opinion, if you are in an organization or industry that is unionized, unions are an important stakeholder in terms of how you are able to influence the empowerment and retention levels of your employees.

CHAPTER 12

The Bottom Line

"Opportunity is missed by most people because it is dressed in overalls and looks like work."

-Thomas Edison

What is a customer?

- Any person or entity that utilizes your organizations products or services.

Why do businesses cater to customers?

- Businesses cater to customers because they make them money.

Why do businesses go into business in the first place?

- Businesses go into business to make a profit.

Why do businesses hire employees?

- To help them serve the customers.

Businesses go into business, hire employees, and serve customers.

Employees make the company money too. Think about it. Companies want long time, preferably lifetime, customers. That kind of secure cash flow is preferable for any business.

How many businesses out there are striving for lifelong employees?

Not every customer is or should be a lifetime customer, nor should every employee be a lifetime employee. But the importance of both a customer and an employee with a lifetime commitment to purchasing or delivering an organizations services is extremely profitable. Customers may be far more willing to patronize an organization if they know the employees are stable. They get to know them, develop a relationship, and continue with that familiar and successful business relationship.

The ideas in this book ask you to consider the disparity between how an organization views its customers versus its employees and how this disparity affects the bottom line.

When we look at the idea of the "triple bottom line" - being profits, people, and planet - it could be argued that the employee has a far greater impact on these things than any individual customer would.

Tullberg (2012) identifies the three value spheres of the triple bottom line as the social, environmental, and economic, and suggests that the challenge for organizations is to fill these general terms with actual substance in order to realize value. He also discusses the subjectivity of some of the metrics in terms of association versus causation of many of the variables involved in analyzing a triple bottom line approach.

It appears that more companies are moving towards some type of triple bottom line approach as a KPMG study cited in Tullberg (2012) showed that 70% of the top 250 companies in the world were doing so by 2005, up 15% from just three years before.

The point here is not to diminish the role of customers. Clearly if there were no customers there would be no organization. But keep this in mind as well, if there were no employees to serve the customers, the result would be the same, and the business would have to close its doors.

An organization could never survive if it simply relied on the fact that there was an endless supply of customers to fill their business needs. Some employers do appear to be taking the approach that there appears to be an endless supply of labor so they put the "customer first". Other organizations, in particularly those that rely on skilled labor, are starting to move towards the direction of trying to attract and retain employees.

I would still argue (and you may disagree) that this existing level of effort to attract and retain employees is still far below the amount of resources that are utilized to attract and retain customers. It is important that this changes for future businesses that wish to remain competitive in their sector.

CHAPTER 13

Conclusions

"Two roads diverged in a wood and I – I took the one less traveled by, and that has made all the difference."

-Robert Frost

You may have heard the saying, or experienced it yourself, that employees seldom leave jobs, they leave supervisors. It is also often the case that employees leave because they didn't like the environment they were working in and leaving had little to do with the nature of the work itself.

What if that applied to your customers, that they liked the product, just not how you treated them or how they felt being in the store so they left and never came back. It sounds like something that shouldn't ever happen to a customer, and businesses go to great lengths to make sure this doesn't happen. But what about employees, they leave due to these reasons all the time and it seems to be accepted as a part of many organizational cultures:

"If you don't like it, leave."

"If you don't do it I'll find someone who will."

"We are paying you to do a job here."

"It's my name on the door so you'll do as I say."

"That's nothing, when I started out things were much worse than they are now, suck it up."

"Employees are entitled and complain too much."

This list could go on and on. I would suggest that if you haven't heard any of these you are in the lucky minority or you have been fortunate to work for great employers.

It's about focusing on process to get the result, not focusing on the result to get the result.

An example that sticks with me listening to fighters and athletes talk about their preparation, is a quote from Muhammad Ali that says:

"The fight is won or lost far away from the witnesses – behind the lines, in the gym, and out there on the road, long before I dance under those lights".

Much of what constitutes good employee and customer service is a result of good preparation and training, again process focused versus results focused.

Are there certain situations where there are customers that you would say no to? Absolutely. Any customer that is abusive to staff, destroys property, steals from your business, you don't want their money or their presence in your workplace. The same goes for employees, but what is true of customers (that 99% of them are customers that you want), is true of employees. Most of them you want to hang on to.

Brooks (2013) writes about 4 key principles that discuss how to treat your staff as you do your customers:

1) Make your customers (staff) successful – Brooks (2013) writes that making your staff successful will make your business successful. He cites that most of us probably think more about what we need to do to be successful, as opposed to thinking about

what our staff need to be successful.

It sounds simple enough, and I think really it is. It could also be looking at as creating a self-fulfilling prophesy. For example believing that your staff are as important as your customers, that they are there to further the business and investing in them the same way the organization invests to attract and retain customers, will be beneficial in the long run. Conversely, believing the opposite or that employees are not as valuable as customers, by not investing in their training and development you may prove yourself right.

2) Put your customers (staff) first – Brooks (2013) cites a disgruntled employee that felt staff came last, and asks that you answer that question. How would your staff answer about where they felt they existed on the priority list of the organization?

You can say all you want about how the organization (or yourself) puts employees as a top priority, but as usual actions speak louder than words.

A first step may be as Dr. Brooks suggests, to simply ask them, and then work towards making sure that they are the organizations top priority.

3) Learn from your customers (staff) – Brooks (2013) asks if you take time to ask your staff about how to improve the customer experience?

Think about companies like Google that cite a number of their top innovations have come directly from employees themselves, and similarly with LinkedIn's [in]cubator program. At Google, employees are expected to spend 20% of their time experimenting with new ideas (Koch, 2014).

Virgin's Sir Richard Branson also cites intra-preneurs as a major reason why Virgin is now composed of a group of 200 companies (Koch, 2014).

4) Walk in your customer's (staff's) shoes – Brooks (2013) cites that it is not human nature to see thing from another person's point of view, and for example if a hammer hits a thumb the only way you will feel the pain is if you are connected to the thumb.

A word of caution here, in that you may not be able to (and most likely in many cases) understand what an employee is thinking or feeling. To say such a thing might be disingenuous.

On a final note, whether you are a manager, employee, owner or customer:

We are all in this together.

References

Ballinger, G., Craig, E., Cross, R., & Gray, P. (2011). A Stitch in Time Saves Nine: Leveraging Networks To Reduce The Costs Of Turnover. *California Management Review, 53*(4), 111-133

Beltramini, R. F. (2011, September). From Platitudes to Principles. *Journal of Advertising Research.* pp. 475-476.

Brooks, I. (2013). Treat Your Staff As Your Customers. *NZ Business, 27*(11), 50.

Burke, B. (Speaker). (2014, January 13). *Red Deer Chamber of Commerce Speaker Series.* Alberta: Red Deer Chamber of Commerce.

Carnegie, D. (1936). *How to Win Friends & Influence People.* New York: Simon and Schuster.

Cascio, W. F. (2012). Risks Of Employee Turnover. *HR Magazine, 57*(4), 40-41.

Coget, J. (2011). Does Managerial Motivation Spill Over to Subordinates?. *Academy Of Management Perspectives, 25*(4), 84-85.

Cogin, J. (2012). Are Generational Differences in Work Values Fact or Fiction? Multi-Country Evidence and Implications. *International Journal Of Human Resource Management, 23*(11), 2268-2294.

Crain, R. (2003). If Consumers Crave Familiar, Bring Back The Golden Oldies. Advertising Age, *74*(16), 20.

Drago, R., Wooden, M., & Black, D. (2009). Who Wants And Gets Flexibility? Changing Work Hours Preferences And Life Events. *Industrial & Labor Relations Review, 62*(3), 394-414.

DuBrin, A. J. (1990). *Winning Office Politics*. New York: Prentice Hall.

Fulmer, I., Gerhant, B., & Scott, K. S. (2003). Are The 100 Best Better? An Empirical Investigation Of The Relationship Between Being A "Great Place To Work" And Firm Performance. *Personnel Psychology, 56*(4), 965-993.

Godard, J., & Frege, C. (2013). Labor Unions, Alternative Forms of Representation, and the Exercise of Authority Relations in U.S. Workplaces. *Industrial & Labor Relations Review, 66*(1), 142-168.

Goodman, T. (1997). *The Forbes Book of Business Quotations – 10,000 Thoughts on the Business of Life*. New York: Black Dog and Leventhal Publishers.

Grant, A. M. (2011). How Customers Can Rally Your Troops. *Harvard Business Review, 89*(6), 96-103.

Ghosh, A. (2013). Employee Empowerment: A Strategic Tool to Obtain Sustainable Competitive Advantage. *International Journal Of Management, 30*(3 Part 1), 95-107.

Herzberg, F. (2003). One More Time: How Do You Motivate Employees?. *Harvard Business Review, 81*(1), 87-96.

Kim, J., Natter, M., & Spann, M. (2009). Pay What You Want: A New Participative Pricing Mechanism. *Journal Of Marketing, 73*(1), 44-58.

Kleiner, A. (2000). Above Platitudes? Yes. *Across The Board, 37*(1), 73.

Koch, C. (2014). The Rise of the Intrapreneur. *Director, 67*(7), 72-73.

Manimala, M. J., & Wasdani, K. (2013). Distributed Leadership at Google. Lessons from the Billion-dollar Brand. *Ivey Business Journal, 77*(3), 12-14.

Nicholson, N. (2003). How to Motivate Your Problem People. *Harvard Business Review, 81*(1), 56-65.

Priyadarshi, P. (2011). Employer Brand Image as Predictor of Employee Satisfaction, Affective Commitment & Turnover. *Indian Journal Of Industrial Relations, 46*(3), 510-522.

Riener, G. Traxler, C. When the Rule is "Pay what you want," Almost Everyone Pays Something. *Harvard Business Review, 90*(10), 28.

Rigby, D. K., & Ledingham, D. (2004). CRM Done Right. *Harvard Business Review, 82*(11), 118-129.

Schaeffer, L. D. (2002). The Leadership Journey. *Harvard Business Review, 80*(10), 42-47.

Sirianni, N. J., Bitner, M., Brown, S. W., & Mandel, N. (2013). Branded Service Encounters: Strategically Aligning Employee Behavior with the Brand Positioning. *Journal Of Marketing, 77*(6), 108-123.

Spady, K. V. (2014). *Third Party Corporate Training – Opportunities and Challenges Facing Small and Medium Sized Businesses in Alberta.* Canada: Avason Consulting Corp.

Spears, V. P. (2011). MIT Sloan Research Shows Retailers Can Invest in Employees and Still Profit. *Employee Benefit Plan Review, 66*(6), 25-26..

Spreier, S. W., Fontaine, M. H., & Malloy, R. L. (2006). Leadership Run Amok. *Harvard Business Review, 84*(6), 72-82.

Tullberg, J. (2012). Triple Bottom Line - A Vaulting Ambition?. *Business Ethics: A European Review, 21*(3), 310-324.

Wilden, R., Gudergan, S., & Lings, I. (2010). Employer Branding: Strategic Implications for Staff Recruitment. *Journal Of Marketing Management, 26*(1/2), 56-73.

Wilkinson, S., Linke, R., Gagne, K., Mitchell, R. L., Pratt, M. K., Abrosio, J., & Stackpole, B. (2014). 100 Best Places To Work In IT 2014. *Computerworld, 48*(11), 13-52.

Zaibak, O. (2010, November 8). 99 Legendary Customer Service Quotes. Retrieved from: http://customerthink.com/99_legendary_customer_service_quotes/

ABOUT THE AUTHOR

Kurt Spady, President & CEO of Avason Consulting, is a management and organizational development consultant and trainer based in Red Deer, Alberta. He has over 10 years of practical management and leadership experience with private and public organizations, unionized workplaces, retail service providers, as well as within healthcare and academic institutions.

Kurt has conducted extensive training and consulting in supervision, communication, human resources, team building, supply chain management, and total quality management with individuals and organizations to help them identify and develop areas for productive change.

He holds a Bachelor of Management degree (BMgmt) with a major in Human Resources, and a Master of Business Administration (MBA) degree from Athabasca University.

Avason Consulting Corp. was founded in 2011 and provides "solutions for higher education" to small and medium sized businesses in both online and classroom formats.

Index

A

ability, 9, 12, 20-22,
    31-32, 65
acceptance, 67
accomplish, 12, 65-66
accountability, 11
achievement, 18
adaptive, 48
administration, 91
advancement, 55, 66
advantage, 6, 21, 26,
    33, 43, 49, 59, 63,
    65-67, 72, 88
advertisements, 55, 58
agreements, 75

altruism, 25
ambition, 16, 89
application, 20-21, 47
arguments, 19
assessment, 68
assumptions, 37
athletes, 17, 84
attitude, 9, 14, 22, 48,
    55, 58, 62, 67, 69
autocratic, 14-15, 68
autonomy, 13, 59, 66,
    71
awareness, 3, 29,
    35-36, 69, 72

B

banal, 11, 14, 16, 35
barrier, 22, 54, 67,
    73, 75
basketball, 57, 61
battleground, 42
behaviors, 50
benchmark, 3, 71
beneficial, 4, 9, 32, 85
bottleneck, 44
bottom line, 55,
    79-80, 89
businesses, 4, 7, 26,
    30, 40, 79-81, 83,
    89, 91

C

campaign, 12, 61, 72
career, 4, 13, 18, 47,
    55
career training, 55
causation, 80

caveat, 29, 50
change management,
    65, 70-71, 73
classroom, 54, 91
clichés, 12, 61
commerce, 54, 87
commitment, 57-58,
    67-68, 80, 89
committees, 72
communication, 8,
    11-12, 35, 60, 62,
    70, 72, 91
companies, 3, 7, 32,
    41-42, 47, 55, 58,
    62, 79-80, 85
compensation, 23
competence, 65,
    67-68
competencies, 69
competition, 13, 47
competitive
    advantage, 6, 21,
    33, 43, 49, 63,
    65-67, 72, 88
competitive
    environment, 31
competitor, 1, 3-4,
    43, 46
complaints, 29, 31

consumers, 32, 87
context, 20, 32, 40
contingency, 24, 30
contingency theory,
    30
contribution, 61, 67
convenience, 60
conversation, 1, 31-32
counterintuitive, 1
counterparts, 55
credibility, 59, 68
culture, 57, 61, 69,
    71, 83
customer motivation,
    29-32
customer relationship
    management, 32,
    89
customer service, 1,
    6-7, 9, 16, 29,
    31-32, 39-40, 46,
    84, 90

D

data, 32, 58
decisions, 14-15, 17,
    23, 26, 31, 41, 50,
    65
departments, 12, 16
depth, 3, 61
development, 7, 32,
    63, 69, 72, 85, 91
differences, 8, 87
direct costs, 2
disclaimers, 16
disparity, 44, 80
dissatisfaction, 20,
    39, 44
disseminated, 16
distinction, 18
dollar, 2-4, 17, 23,
    32, 42, 44, 46, 89
downside, 36
drivers, 22
duties, 12, 49

E

education, 91
efficacy, 67
ego, 68
emergency, 15, 35
emotional, 19, 53,
    61-62, 75
empathy, 20
employee attraction
    and retention, 53
employee customer
    service, 1, 7
employee motivation,
    17-18, 21
employee satisfaction,
    48, 89
employee service, 7,
    9, 13, 16, 22, 24,
    27, 32, 39, 46, 48,
    65, 71
employee training,
    27, 43, 61
employee turnover,
    2-4, 27, 53, 71, 87
employer motivation,
    23-24

employment, 43, 58,
    61, 75
empowerment, 13,
    26-27, 31, 44, 50,
    65-73, 77, 88
enforceable, 61
engagement, 45
enterprise, 31
entitlement, 50
environmental, 80
environments, 21
equipment, 44, 54
esteem needs, 66
expectations, 6, 30,
    49-50
expertise, 3, 42
extrinsic, 17, 21

F

facilities, 54, 57
failure, 44
familiarity, 32-33
families, 17
favorably, 76
feedback, 31, 39-40

financially, 53
findings, 76
fiscal, 11, 72
flexibility, 8, 58-59,
    87
foundational, 12, 16,
    20
framework, 71
friends, 30, 35, 87

H

hockey, 17, 54
hours, 23-25, 55, 57,
    87
HR, 3, 7, 47, 61, 87
human resources, 67,
    91
hygiene factors, 20-21

G

gap, 2, 61, 76
generation, 7-8, 13,
    87
generic, 12
gift, 18
gifted, 18
globalization, 9, 48
goal, 4, 6, 12-14, 16,
    18, 57, 66, 70-72
goal setting, 13, 16,
    71

I

implementation, 15,
    73
implications, 87, 90
importance, 31, 80
improvement, 70
incentive, 25-26, 68
individuals, 19-20,
    22, 59, 91
industrial, 13, 15, 69,
    87-89
industries, 4, 16, 27
information, 15, 63,

67
initiative, 7, 67-72
initiatives, 73
innovations, 85
Insights Colors, 36
intentionally, 7, 55
interaction, 63
internally, 33
internet, 46
intra-preneur, 86
intuitive, 30, 58
investigation, 36, 88
investment, 27, 60, 68

J

job dissatisfaction, 20
job satisfaction, 20,
   58
jobs, 3, 15, 35, 47,
   68, 83

L

labor market, 4, 24
latitude, 25-26
leader, 7, 14-16, 18
leadership, 11, 14-16,
   23, 89, 91
legendary, 90
legitimate, 5, 29-30
lessons, 89
leverage, 27, 87
lifelong, 2, 9, 33, 80
lifetime, 2, 32, 42,
   79-80
loyal, 43, 66
loyalty, 7, 9, 14, 19,
   25, 42-43

M

majority, 7, 9, 30, 39,
   41, 46, 50
management, 12-13,
   22, 30-32, 49-50,

53, 65, 68-71, 73,
  75-76, 87-88, 90-91
managerial, 15, 87
managers, 7, 13-15,
  19, 21, 30-31, 37,
  40, 44, 48, 50, 66
manipulation, 62
margin, 4
marketers, 62
marketing and
  branding, 57
marketplace, 6, 9, 13,
  15, 17, 21, 54
measurable, 12, 70-71
mechanism, 40, 75,
  88
media, 46
mentorship, 57
metric, 70-71, 80
micro, 22, 49
millennials, 8
minority, 42, 44, 84
minutes, 4-7
misguided, 46
mismatch, 4, 22, 24
mission, 49, 60, 69
mistrust, 68
motivation, 17-19,
  21-24, 26-27,
  29-32, 54, 87

motivators, 19-21
Myers Briggs, 36

N

nonconfrontational,
  36

O

obligations, 61
openness, 67
operations, 17, 71
opinions, 36, 39-40,
  58
opportunities, 41, 47,
  55, 63, 66, 89
options, 24, 58
organizational culture,
  61, 69
organizational
  networks, 3

orientated, 4, 8
orientation, 18, 20,
  27, 46, 71
outcomes, 6, 20, 31,
  51
overtime, 23
owners, 50, 53

P

pacesetting, 16
paperwork, 44
pareto principle, 2, 21
participants, 36
paternalistic, 15, 49,
  68
patronize, 80
patrons, 25
paycheck, 9, 41
percentages, 4, 18,
  40, 72
perception, 8, 18-20,
  35, 50, 58-61, 69,
  76
performance, 14, 16,
  19, 31, 55, 66, 88

periods, 8, 24
personality, 36
personality profile, 36
personnel, 88
perspective, 14, 36,
  39-41, 50, 53, 61,
  63, 66, 87
persuasive, 62
pigeonholing, 36
platforms, 46
platitude, 11, 13, 16,
  35, 61-62, 87-88
predictor, 42, 89
preferable, 8, 24, 54,
  79, 87
preparation, 84
presence, 84
president, 17, 44, 54,
  91
priceless, 42
principles, 84, 87
priority, 12, 20, 41,
  63, 69, 85
problems, 11, 44
procedure, 9, 40
production, 19
productive, 13, 21,
  23, 91
productivity, 2, 16, 23

products, 25, 27, 29,
    40, 43, 62, 79
professionals, 8
profile, 3, 36
profitable, 25-26, 80
projection, 60
promotion, 43
provider, 27, 29, 91
psychologists, 36
psychology, 60, 88
publishers, 88

Q

qualifications, 48
quantifiable, 42
quantitative, 70

R

rationale, 2, 5-6, 14,
    25, 45, 48

rationalization, 46
ratios, 55
reactionary, 24
realism, 12
realistic, 19
reality, 6, 20, 50, 58
reasonable, 22, 70
rebuttal, 1, 5-6, 13,
    24, 26
reciprocity, 45
recognition, 65-66
recruitment, 43, 59,
    62, 90
reduction, 27
reformer, 15
refund, 1, 7
regression, 58
relations, 69, 87-89
relationship, 3, 5-6,
    32-33, 43, 51,
    67-68, 76, 80, 88
relationships, 9, 21,
    69, 76
relevant, 12, 32,
    70-72
remorse, 61
repairable, 5
replicate, 33
representation, 75-76,

88
representatives, 72
resources, 2, 11-12,
    40, 67, 70, 72, 81
response, 8, 13, 25
responsibility, 11,
    65-68
restaurant, 25
restitution, 1
restrictive, 75
resume, 3
retail, 91
retailers, 89
retention, 32, 43, 48,
    53, 60, 62, 77
retirement, 24, 50
revenue, 2
roles, 37

S

safety, 23, 76
salary, 2, 5, 20
sales, 27, 32, 47, 55,
    70-71
salespeople, 57
savings, 44

scenarios, 27
seasonal, 4
sector, 59, 81
self-interest, 23
seller, 25
series, 17, 54, 87
service, 90
sessions, 22, 36
shortlisted, 47
skill, 3, 14, 42,
    48-49, 65-66,
    69-70, 81
SMART goals, 13,
    16, 70-71
solution, 1, 5, 27, 44,
    91
speaker, 17, 54, 87
stakeholder, 16, 41,
    71-72, 77
statistics, 2
status, 65-66, 68
strategic, 15, 23, 32,
    65, 88-90
strategic plan, 11
stressors, 19
students, 25
subjectivity, 2, 80
success, 20, 40-42,
    45, 47-48, 62-63,

67, 69, 72-73
suggestions, 3, 11
supervision, 15, 91
supervisor, 37, 44,
    49, 53, 59, 67-69,
    83
sustainability, 23
symptoms, 20
systems, 8, 22, 31-32,
    67, 76

T

tailored, 69
talent, 58
tangible, 12, 50
technology, 31, 46, 48
telecommuting, 58
theft, 6
theory, 13, 20, 30
third party corporate
    training, 89
timeframe, 44
timeline, 12, 70-72
timely, 12, 70-72
trader, 27
traditionalists, 8

trainer, 91
trait, 36
transactional, 15
transformational, 15
transparency, 11-12
treatment, 40, 50, 63
troops, 18, 88
True Colors, 36
truth, 6, 14, 39-40, 60
turnover, 2-4, 27,
    53-54, 58, 71, 87,
    89
turnover rate, 4
two-factor theory, 20

U

unattended, 6
underdelivered, 56
unionization, 75-76
unionized, 75-77, 91
unions, 75-77, 88
unsatisfied, 8, 43
unsuccessful, 47
unwilling, 68

54-55, 58, 69, 75,
84, 88, 91

V

variables, 76, 80
variations, 70
variety, 8, 24, 31, 58
vice, 44
viewpoint, 20
vision, 60, 69
visionary, 16
voluntarily, 3

W

weather, 59
website, 47
widget, 70
work environment, 19
work-life balance,
    7-8, 13, 56
workers, 2-3, 7-8, 13,
    41, 59, 61, 76
workforce, 8
worklife, 20
workplace, 7-8, 17,